Mastering 11+

Vocabulary

Workbook for KS2 and Eleven Plus

ashkraft
EDUCATIONAL

Mastering 11+ © 2015 ashkraft educational

This page is intentionally left blank

Mastering 11+ Vocabulary
Workbook for KS2 and Eleven Plus

ISBN-13: 978-1-910678 091

9 781910 678091

"The most important thing is to read as much as you can, like I did. It will give you an understanding of what makes good writing and it will enlarge your vocabulary."

J. K. Rowling

Section 1

Group Words / Collections

EXERCISE 1: Group Words – Animals

Select the appropriate group word for each animal or bird.

A. Gaggle	B. Herd	C. Litter	D. School	E. Troop
F. Swarm	G. Nest	H. Army	I. Pride	J. Pack

Question Number	Animal / Bird	Answer Option	Write the group word in this column
1	Rabbits	**G**	**Nest**
2	Ants	H	Army
3	Geese	A	Gaggle
4	Butterflies	F	Swarm
5	Wolves	J	Pack
6	Goats	B	Herd
7	Apes	E	Troop
8	Cubs	C	Litter
9	Fish	D	School
10	Lions	I	pride

EXERCISE 2: Group Words – Animals

Select the appropriate group word for each animal or bird.

A. Army	B. Colony	C. Flock	D. Swarm	E. Shoal
F. Memory	G. Congregation	H. Bunch	I. Leash	J. Brood

Question Number	Animal / Bird	Answer Option	Write the group word in this column
1	Alligators	G	Congregation
2	Bats	B	Colony
3	Bees	D	Swarm
4	Chickens	J	Brood
5	Deer	H	Bunch
6	Ducks	C	Flock
7	Elephants	F	Memory
8	Foxes	I	Leash
9	Frogs	A	Army
10	Herring	E	Shoal

EXERCISE 3: Group Words – Animals

Select the appropriate group word for each animal or bird.

A. Herd	B. Plague	C. Pack	D. Nest	E. Flight
F. Muster	G. Troop	H. Stud	I. Kindle	J. Building

Question Number	Animal / Bird	Answer Option	Write the group word in this column
1	Monkeys	G	Troop
2	Buffaloes	A	Herd
3	Rascals	C	Pack
4	Rooks	J	Building
5	Insects	B	Plague
6	Kittens	I	Kindle
7	Mice	D	Nest
8	Peacocks	F	Muster
9	Swallows	E	Flight
10	Horses	H	Stud

EXERCISE 4: Group Words – People

Select the appropriate group word for each type of person.

A. Band	B. Group	C. Class	D. Gang	E. Army
F. Staff	G. Troupe	H. Galaxy	I. Bench	J. Crew

Question Number	Animal / Bird	Answer Option	Write the group word in this column
1	Lawyers	H	Galaxy
2	Students	C	Class
3	Musicians	A	Band
4	Teachers	F	Staff
5	Dancers	G	Troupe
6	Friends	B	Group
7	Sailors	J	Crew
8	Labourers	D	Gang
9	Soldiers	E	Army
10	Bishops	I	Bench

EXERCISE 5: Group Words – Things

Select the appropriate group word for each question.

A. Library	B. Bunch	C. Punnet	D. Galaxy	E. Cluster
F. Skein	G. Sheaf	H. Bundle	I. Bouquet	J. Bunch

Question Number	Thing / Object	Answer Option	Write the group word in this column
1	Bananas	B	Bunch
2	Strawberries	C	punnet
3	Grapes	J	Bunch
4	Stars	D	Galaxy
5	Diamonds	E	cluster
6	Books	A	Library
7	Sticks	H	Bundle
8	Flowers	I	Bouquet
9	Arrows	G	Sheaf
10	Silk	F	Skein

Section 2

Plurals

EXERCISE 6: Plurals

Write the plural for each of the words below.

Question Number	Singular	Plural
1	Radius	Radii
2	Church	Churches
3	Goose	Geese
4	Deer	Deer
5	Child	children
6	Fish	Fish
7	Axis	Axes
8	Oasis	Oases
9	Summary	Summaries
10	Life	Lives

EXERCISE 7: Plurals

Write the plural for each of the words below.

Question Number	Singular	Plural
1	Appendix	Appendices
2	Sheep	Sheep
3	Mouse	Mice
4	Crisis	Crises
5	Fungus	Fungi
6	Criterion	Criteria
7	Medium	Media
8	Ox	Oxen
9	Matrix	Matrices
10	Formula	Formulae

EXERCISE 8: Plurals

Write the plural for each of the words below.

Question Number	Singular	Plural
1	Witness	Witnesses
2	Aircraft	Aircrafts
3	Storey	Storeys
4	Fly	Flies
5	Shelf	Shelves
6	Wife	Wives
7	Tornado	Tornadoes
8	Tomato	Tomatoes
9	Zero	Zeroes
10	Calf	Calves

EXERCISE 9: Plurals

Write the plural for each of the words below.

Question Number	Singular	Plural
1	Passer-by	passers-by
2	Cupful	Cupful (s)
3	Penny	pence
4	Reef	Reefs
5	Piano	Pianos
6	Dwarf	Dwarves
7	Knife	Knives
8	Echo	Echoes
9	Charity	Charities
10	Sister-in-law	Sisters-in-law

EXERCISE 10: Plurals

Write the plural for each of the words below.

Question Number	Singular	Plural
1	Bacterium	Bacteria
2	Diagnosis	Diagnoses
3	Moose	Moose
4	Person	Persons People
5	Die	Dice
6	Datum	Data
7	Lasso	Lassoes
8	Trout	Trout
9	Genius	Genius
10	Phenomenon	Phenomena

Section 3

Gender Words

EXERCISE 11: Feminine words

Match the masculine words to their feminine equivalent.

A. Matron	B. Milkmaid	C. Nun	D. Priestess	E. Countess
F. Spinster	G. Mistress	H. Lass	I. Niece	J. Duchess

Question Number	Masculine word	Answer Option	Corresponding feminine word
1	Monk	C	
2	Duke	J	
3	Governor	A	
4	Milkman	B	
5	Priest	D	
6	Lad	H	
7	Nephew	I	
8	Earl	E	
9	Master	G	
10	Bachelor	F	

EXERCISE 12: Feminine words

Match the feminine words to their masculine equivalent.

A. Masseur	B. Usher	C. Fiancé	D. Shepherd	E. Testator
F. Manservant	G. Governor	H. Wizard	I. Widower	J. Emperor

Question Number	Feminine Word	Answer Option	Corresponding masculine word
1	Empress	J	
2	Fiancée	C	
3	Masseuse	A	
4	Shepherdess	D	
5	Usherette	B	
6	Maidservant	F	
7	Testatrix	E	
8	Widow	I	
9	Witch	H	
10	Matron	G	

Section 4

Parents and their young

EXERCISE 13: Young

Select the appropriate young for each of the adult below.

A. Owlet	B. Cub	C. Leveret	D. Kid	E. Gosling
F. Joey	G. Calf	H. Lamb	I. Foal	J. Piglet

Question Number	Parent	Answer Option	Corresponding Young
1	Camel	G	
2	Fox	B	
3	Goat	D	
4	Horse	I	
5	Owl	A	
6	Hare	C	
7	Sheep	H	
8	Goose	E	
9	Possum	F	
10	Pig	J	

EXERCISE 14: Young

Select the appropriate young for each of the adult below.

A. Grub	B. Squab	C. Calf	D. Tadpole	E. Nymph
F. Caterpillar	G. Hatchling	H. Cygnet	I. Cub	J. Parr

Question Number	Parent	Answer Option	Corresponding Young
1	Ant	A	
2	Swan	H	
3	Pigeon	B	
4	Butterfly	F	
5	Salmon	J	
6	Shark	I	
7	Toad	D	
8	Turtle	G	
9	Whale	C	
10	Grasshopper	E	

EXERCISE 15: Young

Select the appropriate young for each of the adult below.

A. Leveret	B. Fawn	C. Pup	D. Chick	E. Kit
F. Colt	G. Calf	H. Eyas	I. Peachick	J. Pup

Question Number	Parent	Answer Option	Corresponding Young
1	Bat	C	
2	Deer	B	
3	Hare	A	
4	Peafowl	I	
5	Seal	J	
6	Sparrow	D	
7	Donkey	F	
8	Hawk	H	
9	Cattle	G	
10	Weasel	E	

Section 5

Homophones

EXERCISE 16: Homophones

Select the word that matches the description of each phrase/word.

A. Principle	B. Queue	C. Principal	D. Current	E. Discreet
F. Discrete	G. Cue	H. Currant	I. Complacent	J. Complaisant

Question Number	Description	Answer
1	Provide signal for action	Cue
2	Line of people	Queue
3	An important rule	Pri Principal
4	Head of an educational institute	Principal
5	Being careful in one's speech or action	Discreet
6	Individually separate and distinct	Discrete
7	A small dried fruit	Currant
8	Flow of electricity	Current
9	Being content with oneself	Complacent
10	Willing to please others	G

EXERCISE 17: Homophones

Select the word that matches the description of each phrase/word.

A. Right	B. Practice	C. Sight	D. Holy	E. Seer
F. Practise	G. Wholly	H. Sear	I. Cite	J. Rite

Question Number	Description	Answer
1	Entirely	G
2	Sacred	D
3	A ritual or a ceremony	J
4	Correct as a fact	A
5	To see or observe	C
6	Refer to a passage or book	I
7	Perform an action	F
8	A custom or tradition	B
9	A person who can see the future	E
10	Burning sensation	H

EXERCISE 18:   Homophones

Select the word that matches the description of each phrase/word.

A. Aural	B. Lone	C. Wreath	D. Envelop	E. Sceptic
F. Septic	G. Loan	H. Envelope	I. Oral	J. Wreathe

Question Number	Description	Answer
1	Spoken and not written	I
2	Having no companion	B
3	Borrow something	G
4	Sense of hearing	A
5	Surround or encircle	J
6	Cover something	D
7	A circle-shaped arrangement of flowers	C
8	A paper container	H
9	Doubtful	E
10	Infected wound	F

EXERCISE 19: Homophones

Select the word that matches the description of each phrase/word.

A. Desert	B. Dessert	C. Complement	D. Kerb	E. Dual
F. Curb	G. Duel	H. Compliment	I. Council	J. Counsel

Question Number	Description	Answer
1	Sweet dish at the end of a meal	B
2	Praise or admire someone	H
3	Stone edging of a raised path	D
4	Consisting of two parts	E
5	Abandon someone or something	A
6	Formal advice	J
7	A meeting for discussion	I
8	Restrain	F
9	Supplement	C
10	Contest or fight	G

EXERCISE 20: Homophones

Select the word that matches the description of each phrase/word.

A. Stationary	B. Forbear	C. Forebear	D. Sweet	E. Suite
F. Palate	G. Palette	H. Chord	I. Cord	J. Stationery

Question Number	Description	Answer
1	A set of rooms	E
2	An ancestor	C
3	Materials used for writing	J
4	Plate used to mix colours	G
5	Not moving	A
6	A group of musical notes	H
7	Taste of sugar or honey	D
8	Taste buds	F
9	Thin rope	I
10	Hold back	B

Section 6

Homes / Habitat

EXERCISE 21: Homes - Persons

Select the traditional home for each question from the table below.

A. Prison	B. Temple	C. Barracks	D. Hospital	E. Monastery
F. Caravan	G. Cottage	H. Tent	I. Vicarage	J. Convent

Question Number	Person	Answer Option	Write the answer in this column
1	Nun	J	
2	Nomad	H	
3	Convict	A	
4	Gypsy	F	
5	Monk	E	
6	Priest	B	
7	Peasant	G	
8	Patient	D	
9	Soldier	C	
10	Vicar	I	

EXERCISE 22: Homes – Creatures

Select the traditional home for each question from the table below.

A. Pen	B. Lair	C. Kennel	D. Web	E. Lodge
F. Den	G. Holt	H. Hive	I. Stable	J. Nest

Question Number	Person	Answer Option	Write the answer in this column
1	Spider	D	
2	Beaver	E	
3	Ant	J	
4	Otter	G	
5	Bee	H	
6	Dog	C	
7	Horse	I	
8	Bear	F	
9	Sheep	A	
10	Lion	B	

EXERCISE 23: Homes – Creatures

Select the traditional home for each question from the table below.

A. Byre	B. Drey	C. Shell	D. Form	E. Sett
F. Coop	G. Lair	H. Dovecote	I. Soil	J. Nest

Question Number	Person	Answer Option	Write the answer in this column
1	Fowl	F	
2	Squirrel	B	
3	Snail	C	
4	Mouse	J	
5	Pigeon	H	
6	Fox	G	
7	Hare	D	
8	Badger	E	
9	Cow	A	
10	Earthworm	I	

Section 7

Spellings

EXERCISE 24: Incorrect Spelling

Write the correct spelling for each of the words listed below.

Question Number	Word spelt incorrectly	Write the correct spelling in this column
1	beleive	believe
2	tommorrow	tomorrow
3	agression	aggression
4	arguement	argument
5	accomodate	accommodate
6	chauffer	chauffeur
7	embarass	embarrass
8	ecstacy	ecstasy
9	necessury	necessary
10	cemetary	Cemetery

EXERCISE 25: Incorrect Spelling

Write the correct spelling for each of the words listed below.

Question Number	Word spelt incorrectly	Write the correct spelling in this column
1	persistant	persistent
2	unfortunatly	unfortunately
3	supercede	supersede
4	occuring	occurring
5	tendancy	tendency
6	liase	
7	irresistable	
8	humourous	
9	harrassment	
10	independant	

Mastering 11+ / VOCABULARY / Practice Book

Section 8

Synonyms

EXERCISE 26: Synonyms

Select the word that has the same or closest meaning to the primary word.
There is only one correct answer for each question.

A. Patronise	B. Sincere	C. Unhappiness	D. Massive	E. Ultimate
F. Wither	G. Unfertile	H. Grab	I. Control	J. Repent

Question Number	Primary word	Answer Option	Write the answer in this column
1	DISCONTENT	C	
2	SEIZE	H	
3	STOOP	A	
4	EARNEST	B	
5	WILT	F	
6	ATONE	J	
7	BARREN	G	
8	IMMENSE	D	
9	IDEAL	E	
10	RESTRAINT	I	

EXERCISE 27: Synonyms

Select the word that has the same or closest meaning to the primary word.
There is only one correct answer for each question.

A. Withstand	B. Stake	C. Withdraw	D. Pilot	E. Direct
F. Female	G. Quill	H. Determined	I. Track	J. Reserved

Question Number	Primary word	Answer Option	Write the answer in this column
1	OBSTINATE	H	
2	ABSTAIN	C	
3	WEATHER	A	
4	WAGER	B	
5	TRAIL	I	
6	TRIAL	D	
7	NAVIGATE	E	
8	FEMININE	F	
9	FEATHER	G	
10	FROSTY	J	

EXERCISE 28: Synonyms

Select the word that has the same or closest meaning to the primary word.
There is only one correct answer for each question.

A. Swagger	B. Beard	C. Antique	D. Fairness	E. Imaginary
F. Growth	G. Autocracy	H. Clothing	I. Countless	J. Bandit

Question Number	Primary word	Answer Option	Write the answer in this column
1	ARROGANCE	A	
2	ATTIRE	H	
3	STUBBLE	B	
4	PROGRESS	F	
5	PIRATE	J	
6	JUSTICE	D	
7	VINTAGE	C	
8	MYTHICAL	E	
9	MYRIAD	I	
10	TYRANNY	G	

EXERCISE 29: Synonyms

Select the word that has the same or closest meaning to the primary word.

There is only one correct answer for each question.

A. Relaxed	B. Fatal	C. Shield	D. Inner	E. Unsure
F. Flop	G. Mediocre	H. Puzzle	I. Shy	J. Perfume

Question Number	Primary word	Answer Option	Write the answer in this column
1	DUBIOUS	E	
2	CAREFREE	A	
3	ARMOUR	C	
4	TERMINAL	B	
5	FAILURE	F	
6	FRAGRANCE	J	
7	INTERIOR	D	
8	INFERIOR	G	
9	INTROVERT	I	
10	PARADOX	H	

EXERCISE 30: Synonyms

Select the word that has the same or closest meaning to the primary word.
There is only one correct answer for each question.

A. Soil	B. Avoid	C. Fluctuate	D. Ardent	E. Enormous
F. Relief	G. Honesty	H. Lawyer	I. Whisper	J. Steam

Question Number	Primary word	Answer Option	Write the answer in this column
1	MURMUR	I	
2	RESPITE	F	
3	FERVENT	D	
4	OSCILLATE	C	
5	CIRCUMVENT	B	
6	BARRISTER	H	
7	INTEGRITY	G	
8	GIGANTIC	E	
9	VAPOUR	J	
10	EARTH	A	

EXERCISE 31: Synonyms

Select the word that has the same or closest meaning to the primary word.
There is only one correct answer for each question.

A. Fixed	B. Learned	C. Chirpy	D. Lodge	E. Ridiculous
F. Pitiless	G. Support	H. Mutable	I. Sapphire	J. Junk

Question Number	Primary word	Answer Option	Write the answer in this column
1	VARIABLE	H	
2	IMMOBILE	A	
3	VICARAGE	D	
4	VIVACIOUS	C	
5	SAGACIOUS	B	
6	ABSURD	E	
7	CALLOUS	F	
8	GANTRY	G	
9	SPAM	J	
10	INDIGO	I	

EXERCISE 32: Synonyms

Select the word that has the same or closest meaning to the primary word.
There is only one correct answer for each question.

A. Caring	B. Clay	C. Tenure	D. Unclear	E. Indigo
F. Irritating	G. Surplus	H. Honourable	I. Motivation	J. Evil

Question Number	Primary word	Answer Option	Write the answer in this column
1	TERM	C	Tenure
2	BENIGN	H	
3	MALIGNANT	J	
4	NEBULOUS	D	
5	INCENTIVE	I	
6	SCRUPULOUS	A	
7	PRICKLY	F	
8	AZURE	E	
9	CERAMIC	B	
10	EXCESS	G	

EXERCISE 33: Synonyms

Select the word that has the same or closest meaning to the primary word.

There is only one correct answer for each question.

A. Ghost	B. Disobey	C. Betrayal	D. Liberty	E. Lively
F. Coalition	G. Cheerful	H. Weak	I. Jobless	J. Rapid

Question Number	Primary word	Answer Option	Write the answer in this column
1	FREEDOM	D	
2	ALLIANCE	F	
3	TREASON	C	
4	SWIFT	J	
5	REDUNDANT	I	
6	FAINT	H	
7	JOVIAL	G	
8	MERCURIAL	E	
9	FLOUT	B	
10	PHANTOM	A	

EXERCISE 34: Synonyms

Select the word that has the same or closest meaning to the primary word.

There is only one correct answer for each question.

A. Dominance	B. Blanket	C. Filling	D. Astonish	E. Striking
F. Alternative	G. Poor	H. Rational	I. Colourful	J. Stingy

Question Number	Primary word	Answer Option	Write the answer in this column
1	VARIANT	F	
2	FLABBERGAST	D	
3	PRAGMATIC	H	
4	FLAMBOYANT	E	
5	ASCENDANCY	A	
6	STRAPPED	G	
7	MEASLY	J	
8	HEARTY	C	
9	SALIENT	I	
10	QUILT	B	

EXERCISE 35: Synonyms

Select the word that has the same or closest meaning to the primary word.

There is only one correct answer for each question.

A. Alluring	B. Cord	C. Obscure	D. Astonish	E. Wanted
F. Split	G. Rinse	H. Silly	I. Miracle	J. Mixed

Question Number	Primary word	Answer Option	Write the answer in this column
1	RUPTURE	F	
2	TEMPTING	A	
3	WELCOME	E	
4	CONCEAL	C	
5	MARVEL	I	
6	AMAZE	D	
7	GARGLE	G	
8	TRIFLING	H	
9	LACED	J	
10	STRING	B	

Section 9

Antonyms

EXERCISE 36: Antonyms

Select the word that has the opposite meaning to the primary word.

There is only one correct answer for each question.

A. Degrade	B. Order	C. Prolonged	D. Clumsy	E. Haphazard
F. Dire	G. Rude	H. Whisper	I. Horizontal	J. Fasten

Question Number	Primary word	Answer Option	Write the answer in this column
1	CLAMOUR	H	
2	DIGNIFY	A	
3	BRIEF	C	
4	AGILE	D	
5	MARVELLOUS	F	
6	VERTICAL	I	
7	METHODICAL	E	
8	ANARCHY	B	
9	COURTEOUS	G	
10	DETACH	J	

EXERCISE 37: Antonyms

Select the word that has the opposite meaning to the primary word.

There is only one correct answer for each question.

A. Attack	B. Attach	C. Interior	D. Restricted	E. Ally
F. Denote	G. Reward	H. Eternal	I. Blissful	J. Kind

Question Number	Primary word	Answer Option	Write the answer in this column
1	DETACH	B	
2	DEFENCE	A	
3	RIVAL	E	
4	MORTAL	H	
5	EXTERIOR	C	
6	PENALTY	G	
7	EPIDEMIC	D	
8	VICIOUS	J	
9	CONNOTE	F	
10	MISERABLE	I	

Mastering 11+ / VOCABULARY / Practice Book

EXERCISE 38: Antonyms

Select the word that has the opposite meaning to the primary word.
There is only one correct answer for each question.

A. Sturdy	B. Pleased	C. Irritating	D. Listless	E. Vigorous
F. New	G. Weak	H. Separation	I. Apathy	J. Clarity

Question Number	Primary word	Answer Option	Write the answer in this column
1	FUSION	H	
2	FRAGILE	A	
3	VIBRANT	D	
4	VINTAGE	F	
5	SOOTHING	C	
6	LIVID	D	
7	AUTHORITATIVE	G	
8	ENTERPRISE	I	
9	VAGUENESS	J	
10	LANGUID	E	

EXERCISE 39: Antonyms

Select the word that has the opposite meaning to the primary word.

There is only one correct answer for each question.

A. Buyer	B. Attract	C. Fail	D. Working	E. Foolish
F. Rosy	G. Invisible	H. Friend	I. Dispassionate	J. Conceal

Question Number	Primary word	Answer Option	Write the answer in this column
1	ANTAGONIST	H	
2	QUALIFY	C	
3	ARDENT	I	
4	RETIRED	D	
5	SAGACIOUS	E	
6	VENDOR	A	
7	REPEL	B	
8	PALE	F	
9	OBSERVABLE	G	
10	REVEAL	J	

EXERCISE 40: Antonyms

Select the word that has the opposite meaning to the primary word.
There is only one correct answer for each question.

A. Central	B. Mundane	C. Admiration	D. Criticism	E. Lethargic
F. Crucial	G. Cowardice	H. Excitable	I. Evil	J. Shy

Question Number	Primary word	Answer Option	Write the answer in this column
1	PLACID	H	
2	PERIPHERAL	A	
3	MARGINAL	F	
4	MIRACULOUS	B	
5	BRAVADO	G	
6	GREGARIOUS	J	
7	CONTEMPT	C	
8	GOOD	I	
9	PRAISE	D	
10	ENERGETIC	E	

EXERCISE 41: Antonyms

Select the word that has the opposite meaning to the primary word.

There is only one correct answer for each question.

A. Distinguished	B. Minute	C. Order	D. Smart	E. Steady
F. Stupid	G. Ecstasy	H. Truthfulness	I. External	J. Pristine

Question Number	Primary word	Answer Option	Write the answer in this column
1	RUSTY	J	
2	DECEPTION	H	
3	AGONY	G	
4	WOBBLY	E	
5	ANARCHY	C	
6	RAGGED	D	
7	BRAINY	F	
8	INTERNAL	I	
9	ENORMOUS	B	
10	ANONYMOUS	A	

EXERCISE 42: Antonyms

Select the word that has the opposite meaning to the primary word. There is only one correct answer for each question.

A. Capture	B. Bravery	C. Calm	D. Incompetent	E. Careless
F. Robust	G. Varying	H. Precise	I. Stranded	J. Departure

Question Number	Primary word	Answer Option	Write the answer in this column
1	METICULOUS	E	
2	PANIC	C	
3	FRIGHT	B	
4	EFFICIENT	D	
5	CONSISTENT	F	
6	NEBULOUS	H	
7	ARRIVAL	J	
8	RESCUED	A	
9	LIBERATE	I	
10	FEEBLE	B	

EXERCISE 43: Antonyms

Select the word that has the opposite meaning to the primary word. There is only one correct answer for each question.

A. Honest	B. Acquired	C. Uniformity	D. Cowardly	E. Firm
F. Dip	G. Pleasant	H. Summer	I. Unusual	J. Tidy

Question Number	Primary word	Answer Option	Write the answer in this column
1	DIVERSITY	C	
2	PEAK	F	
3	FLOPPY	E	
4	WINTER	H	
5	INTRINSIC	B	
6	INTREPID	D	
7	HABITUAL	I	
8	SLOPPY	J	
9	SNEAKY	A	
10	HORRID	G	

EXERCISE 44: Antonyms

Select the word that has the opposite meaning to the primary word. There is only one correct answer for each question.

A. Insufficient	B. Dated	C. Trounced	D. Brighten	E. Irrational
F. Traditional	G. Wintry	H. Shy	I. Contained	J. Success

Question Number	Primary word	Answer Option	Write the answer in this column
1	FAILURE	J	
2	RAMPANT	I	
3	EXTROVERT	H	
4	BALMY	G	
5	MODERN	F	
6	SCIENTIFIC	E	
7	DARKEN	D	
8	VICTORIOUS	C	
9	CURRENT	B	
10	AMPLE	A	

EXERCISE 45: Antonyms

Select the word that has the opposite meaning to the primary word. There is only one correct answer for each question.

A. Alternate	B. Safe	C. Submit	D. Matching	E. Stylish
F. Pinnacle	G. Measly	H. Naive	I. Terrestrial	J. Employer

Question Number	Primary word	Answer Option	Write the answer in this column
1	CONSECUTIVE	A	
2	AERIAL	I	
3	TACKY	E	
4	OPPOSITE	D	
5	RESIST	C	
6	NADIR	F	
7	PRECARIOUS	B	
8	CYNICAL	H	
9	LIBERAL	G	
10	SERVANT	J	

Section 10

Compound Words

EXERCISE 46: Compound Words

Match the primary word to an appropriate word from the table below to make a compound word. The first question has been answered for you.

A. LET	B. ANT	C. ICE	D. CUP	E. RANT
F. CAST	G. LOCK	H. RED	I. SOME	J. RIDGE

Question Number	Primary Word	Answer	Compound Word
1	QUAD	E	QUADRANT
2	TRIP	A	TRIPLET
3	STIR	A	STIRRED
4	RAMP	D	RAMPANT
5	GRID	G	GRIDLOCK
6	HAND	I	HANDSOME
7	FORE	F	FORECAST
8	JUST	C	JUSTISCE
9	BUTTER	D	BUTTERCUP
10	CART	J	CARTRIDGE

EXERCISE 47: Compound Words

Match the primary word to an appropriate word from the table below to make a compound word.

A. LEDGE	B. LOAD	C. AGE	D. GROUND	E. TUNE
F. JURY	G. FRONT	H. HELD	I. LET	J. HEM

Question Number	Primary Word	Answer	Compound Word
1	KNOW	A	
2	DOWN		
3	UP	H	
4	BACK	D	
5	ANT	J	ANTHEM
6	POST	C	POSTAGE
7	IN	F	
8	FORE	E	FORETUNE
9	OUT	I	OUTLET
10	FOR	G	FOREFRONT

EXERCISE 48: Compound Words

Match the primary word to an appropriate word from the table below to make a compound word.

A. HEM	B. HER	C. ABLE	D. FRINGE	E. LYING
F. WARD	G. ROOT	H. SING	I. TEMPT	J. HORN

Question Number	Primary Word	Answer	Compound Word
1	AT	I	
2	FOR	F	
3	TEA	H	
4	PORT	C	
5	WIT	B	
6	IN	D	
7	OUT	E	
8	MAY	A	
9	GREEN	J	
10	BEET	G	

EXERCISE 49: Compound Words

Match the primary word to an appropriate word from the table below to make a compound word.

A. CONSIDERATE	B. LESS	C. ORE	D. PIES	E. LAW
F. DIVISION	G. MOST	H. HOLD	I. RUST	J. LIFE

Question Number	Primary Word	Answer	Compound Word
1	REST	B	
2	FORE	G	
3	IN	I	
4	THOUGHT	C	
5	OUT	E	
6	WILD	J	
7	BE	H	
8	POP	D	
9	SUB	F	
10	MIST	A	

EXERCISE 50: Compound Words

Match the primary word to an appropriate word from the table below to make a compound word.

A. TRESS	B. PET	C. MARK	D. HOLD	E. CHAT
F. ADEQUACY	G. JET	H. FIRE	I. DON	J. WAG

Question Number	Primary Word	Answer	Compound Word
1	FOR	A	
2	HALL	C	
3	STRONG	D	
4	BACK	H	
5	IN	F	
6	CAR	B	
7	CHIN	J	
8	PAR	I	
9	CHIT	E	
10	INK	G	

Section 11

Idioms

EXERCISE 51: Idioms

Match each idiom to the correct explanation.

Question Number	Idiom/Saying	Answer		Answer Key	Explanation
1	**Put a sock in it**	G		A	Prepare to work harder.
2	Roll up your sleeves	A		B	To be quiet about something.
3	Keep your shirt on	I		C	Instantaneous act or decision making
4	Knickers in a twist	J		D	Having something special for difficult times.
5	Take one's hat off	H		E	Pretending to be harmless when you are really dangerous
6	At the drop of a hat	C		F	To be extremely busy
7	Wolf in sheep's clothing	E		G	**Ask someone to shut up.**
8	Keep it zipped	B		H	Showing respect or admiration
9	Bursting at the seams	F		I	Asking someone to not lose their temper.
10	Card up your sleeve	D		J	Getting upset or confused

EXERCISE 52: Idioms

Match each idiom to the correct explanation.

Question Number	Idiom/Saying	Answer		Answer Key	Explanation
1	Off-the-cuff	I		A	Doing something without any preparation.
2	To dress someone down	G		B	To start thinking seriously about resolving a problem
3	Fit like a glove	A		C	Indicates someone to be very angry.
4	Mutton dressed as lamb	D		D	To be dressed too young for your age.
5	To have a bee in your bonnet	J		E	Describe something that fits very well.
6	Dressed to kill	H		F	To be overdressed for the occasion
7	To be hand in glove	E		G	Telling someone off.
8	To put on your thinking cap	B		H	Looking really good in the clothes you are wearing
9	Dressed up like a dog's dinner	F		I	Having a very close relationship
10	Hot under the collar	C		J	To be obsessed about someone or something

EXERCISE 53: Idioms

Match each idiom to the correct explanation.

Question Number	Idiom/Saying	Answer		Answer Key	Explanation
1	Barking up the wrong tree	F		A	Working late into night
2	Burning the midnight oil	A		B	It is your decision to make
3	Add insult to injury	D		C	Doing a bad job to save money
4	Best of both worlds	E		D	To worsen someone's current situation
5	Every cloud has a silver lining	J		E	Describing a situation where it is all advantages
6	Don't give up the day job	G		F	Accusing the wrong person
7	Feel a bit under the weather	I		G	Telling someone they are not good at something
8	Hit the sack	H		H	Go to sleep
9	Ball is in your court	B		I	Feeling slightly unwell
10	Cut corners	C		J	Being optimistic when the times are tough

EXERCISE 54: Idioms

Match the idiom to the correct explanation.

Question Number	Idiom/Saying	Answer		Answer Key	Explanation
1	It takes two to tango	J		A	Something very easy to do
2	Jump on the bandwagon	G		B	Not knowing the answer to a question
3	Elvis has left the building	H		C	Meaning everything or all of it
4	Piece of cake	A		D	Directly to the point ignoring all the details
5	Sit on the fence	I		E	Used when someone you are talking about arrives
6	Your guess is as good as mine	B		F	When someone is in full control of the situation
7	Speak of the devil	E		G	Joining in an activity
8	The whole nine yards	C		H	It's all over
9	On the ball	F		I	Unable to make a clear decision
10	To make a long story short	D		J	Something needing more than one person to accomplish

EXERCISE 55: Idioms

Match the idiom to the correct explanation.

Question Number	Idiom/Saying	Answer		Answer Key	Explanation
1	Once in a blue moon	G		A	Deceiving other people to think well of them
2	See eye to eye	J		B	Disclosing hidden information
3	Taste of your own medicine	E		C	Someone has missed his or her chance
4	Put wool over other people's eyes	A		D	Not risking everything your have, in one go
5	Two birds with one stone	H		E	Something you've done to others, happen to you
6	Let the cat out of the bag	B		F	Doing or saying something exactly right
7	Miss the boat	C		G	Something that happens very rarely
8	Don't put all your eggs in one basket	D		H	Indicates where people are agreement
9	Curiosity killed the cat	I		I	Prying can lead you into trouble
10	Hit the nail on the head	F		J	Accomplish two goals at once

Section 12

Odd One Out

EXERCISE 56: Odd One Out

Select the word that does not belong to the group.

The first question has been answered for you.

Question Number	A	B	C	D	E	Answer
1	Spring	Sprint	Summer	Winter	Autumn	B
2	Azure	Navy	Indigo	Colt	Cobalt	D
3	Emperor	Fiancé	Lord	Goddess	Mayor	B
4	Stable	Den	Web	Inuit	Parsonage	D
5	Inspire	Bore	Enthuse	Stimulate	Motive	B
6	Germany	Portugal	Spain	India	Italy	D
7	Tomato	Cucumber	Apple	Orange	Banana	B
8	Gang	Pride	Flock	Gaggle	Bandit	E
9	Library	Pack	Clump	Crate	Trace	E
10	Priest	Lady	Queen	Bride	Spinster	A

EXERCISE 57: Odd One Out

Select the word that does not belong to the group.

Question Number	A	B	C	D	E	Answer
1	Sarcastic	Respectful	Ironic	Cynical	Derisive	B
2	Wicket	Cricket	Bat	Stumps	Runs	E
3	Nebulous	Vague	Hazy	Mercurial	Unclear	D
4	Acne	Pinnacle	Summit	Peak	Acme	A
5	Triangle	Rectangle	Square	Sphere	Circle	D
6	Axis	Alliance	Axes	League	Bloc	C
7	Vile	Awful	Admirable	Hateful	Abominable	C
8	Entrap	Trap	Drop	Deceive	Catch	C
9	Century	Decade	Era	Period	Method	E
10	Aviation	Flight	Freight	Fright	Aeronautical	D

EXERCISE 58: Odd One Out

Select the word that does not belong to the group.

Question Number	A	B	C	D	E	Answer
1	Ascend	Rice	Rise	Arise	Mount	B
2	Alien	Foreign	Martian	Martial	Unknown	D
3	Amazon	Everest	Nile	Thames	Ganges	B
4	Tomato	Apple	Banana	Grapes	Potato	E
5	India	Brussels	Brazil	Portugal	Spain	B
6	Aroma	Scene	Odour	Fragrance	Scent	B
7	Interim	Perpetual	Undying	Eternal	Constant	A
8	a	e	i	y	u	D
9	Ambience	Amber	Feel	Tone	Setting	B
10	Minor	Marginal	Pity	Small	Petty	C

EXERCISE 59: Odd One Out

Select the word that does not belong to the group.

Question Number	A	B	C	D	E	Answer
1	Euro	Yen	Rupee	Dollar	Pence	B
2	Bull	Buck	Boar	Doe	Drone	E
3	Glow	Spark	Sprinkle	Radiance	Spark	D
4	Obedient	Meek	Docile	Compliant	Defiant	E
5	Jupiter	Mercurial	Venus	Mars	Saturn	B
6	Ostrich	Otter	Owl	Nightingale	Pigeon	B
7	Calf	Pup	Sow	Kit	Cub	C
8	Reside	Select	Opt	Decide	Elect	A
9	Porch	Entrance	Doorway	Enter	Entryway	A
10	Elicit	Choice	Exclusive	Best	Elite	A

EXERCISE 60: Odd One Out

Select the word that does not belong to the group.

Question Number	A	B	C	D	E	Answer
1	Mars	Mercury	Neptune	Pluto	Jupiter	D
2	Rich	Push	Lush	Posh	Lavish	B
3	French	Danish	English	German	Spanish	D
4	Trauma	Strain	Drama	Ordeal	Shock	
5	Stallion	Mare	Pony	Colt	Bolt	
6	Puppy	Lamb	Sheep	Foal	Kid	C
7	Indigo	Navy	Army	Sapphire	Azure	C
8	Con	Fraud	Trick	Cheat	Pro	E
9	Glimmer	Shimmer	Twinkle	Gleam	Spark	E
10	Portugal	Italy	India	Greece	Spain	D

Section 13

Similes

EXERCISE 61: Similes

Select a word that best completes each simile. The first one has been answered for you.

A. Swan	B. Bone	C. Mouse	D. Sheet	E. Ox
F. Parrot	G. Pig	H. Hawk	I. Owl	J. Bee

Question Number	Simile	Answer
1	As swift as a **Hawk**	**H**
2	As strong as an _____	E
3	As fat as a _____	G
4	As graceful as a _____	A
5	As dry as a _____	B
6	As white as a _____	D
7	As busy as a _____	J
8	As wise as an _____	I
9	As sick as a _____	F
10	As quiet as a _____	C

EXERCISE 62: Similes

Select a word that best completes each simile.

A. Bat	B. Night	C. Lion	D. Razor	E. Lion
F. Fox	G. Peas	H. Solomon	I. Apostle	J. Snail

Question Number	Simile	Answer
1	As fierce as a _____	C
2	As black as a _____	B
3	As cunning as a _____	F
4	As sharp as a _____	D
5	As blind as a _____	A
6	As slow as a _____	J
7	As wise as a _____	H
8	As brave as a _____	E
9	As loyal as an _____	I
10	As alike as two _____ in a pod	G

EXERCISE 63: Similes

Select a word that best completes each simile.

A. Jelly	B. Fruitcake	C. Daisy	D. Rock	E. Hatter
F. Pancake	G. Eel	H. Life	I. Gold	J. Lamb

Question Number	Simile	Answer
1	As flat as a _____	F
2	As mad as a _____	E
3	As innocent as a _____	J
4	As good as _____	I
5	As nutty as _____	B
6	As fresh as a _____	C
7	As difficult as nailing _____ to a tree	A
8	As slipper as an _____	G
9	As large as _____	H
10	As steady as a _____	D

EXERCISE 64: Similes

Select a word that best completes each simile. The first one has been answered for you.

A. Lightning	B. Board	C. Oak	D. Snow	E. Toast
F. Vinegar	G. Bear	H. Hornet	I. Pie	J. Giraffe

Question Number	Simile	Answer
1	As quick as _____	A
2	As stiff as a _____	B
3	As sturdy as an _____	C
4	As white as _____	D
5	As sour as _____	F
6	As tall as _____	J
7	As warm as _____	E
8	As sweet as _____	I
9	As hungry as a _____	G
10	As mad as a _____	H

EXERCISE 65: Similes

Select a word that best completes each simile. The first one has been answered for you.

A. Sleep	B. Sing	C. Act	D. Run	E. Eat
F. Fight	G. Racing	H. Soar	I. Meandered	J. Work

Question Number	Simile	Answer
1	_____ like a pig	C
2	_____ like an angel	B
3	_____ like a dog	G
4	_____ like cats and dogs	F
5	_____ like an animal	E
6	_____ like an eagle	H
7	_____ like a frightened rabbit	J
8	_____ like a hare	D
9	_____ like a stream	I
10	_____ like a log	A

Section 14

Occupations

EXERCISE 66: OCCUPATION

Match each of the following words to the appropriate occupation.
The first one has been done for you.

A. Spanner	B. Rifle	C. Plough	D. Barber	E. Lancet
F. Ward	G. Barrow	H. Glasscutter	I. Brush	J. Prescription

Question Number	Occupation	Answer Choice	Write your answer here.
1	Farmer	C	Plough
2	Mechanic	A	
3	Surgeon	E	
4	Pharmacist	J	
5	Soldier	B	
6	Nurse	F	
7	Glazier	H	
8	Gardener	G	
9	Artist	I	
10	Scissors	D	

EXERCISE 67: OCCUPATION

Match each of the following words to the appropriate occupation.

A. Baton	B. Chimneys	C. Cleaver	D. Mail	E. Plane
F. Car	G. Cutter	H. Anvil	I. Luggage	J. Wig

Question Number	Occupation	Answer Choice	Write your answer here.
1	Postman	D	
2	Blacksmith	H	
3	Policeman	A	
4	Carpenter	E	
5	Judge	J	
6	Butcher	C	
7	Chauffeur	F	
8	Locksmith	G	
9	Porter	I	
10	Steeplejack	B	

EXERCISE 68: OCCUPATION

Match each of the following occupations to the appropriate description.

A. Shopkeeper	B. Postman	C. Reporter	D. Lawyer	E. Mason
F. Magistrate	G. Engineer	'H. Explorer	I. Teacher	J. Priest

Question Number	Occupation	Answer Choice
1	A public officer who deals with matters of law	F
2	A person running a small shop	A
3	Someone delivering mails and parcels	B
4	Someone who build houses	E
5	A person who has studied law and can represent others in a court of law	D
6	A person who writes news articles for a newspaper	C
7	Someone managing and running services at a church or temple	J
8	A person skilled in handling machinery	G
9	A person who travels with the aim of discovering new things and places	H
10	A person helping children acquire new knowledge and skills	I

Mastering 11+ / VOCABULARY / Practice Book

EXERCISE 69: OCCUPATION

Match each of the following occupations to the appropriate description.

A. Carpenter	B. Nurse	C. Dentist	D. Blacksmith	E. Glazier
F. Jockey	G. Secretary	H. Sailor	I. Hacker	J. Pharmacist

Question Number	Occupation	Answer Choice
1	Someone proficient in fitting glass in windows	E
2	Someone experienced in providing medicines	J
3	A person who makes things with iron (metal)	D
4	A person who breaks into computers and computer programs	I
5	A person who deals with woodcraft	A
6	The rider of horses in races	F
7	Someone who helps a manager run his office efficiently	G
8	Someone who cares for sick people	B
9	Someone who works on a ship	H
10	A professional who helps us look after our teeth and gums	C

Section 15

Miscellaneous

EXERCISE 70: CONTAINERS / RECEPTACLES

Match the each of the following containers with their corresponding items.

A. Juice	B. Wine	C. Tea	D. Strawberries	E. Ashes
F. Knife	G. Clothes	H. Money	I. Books	J. Milk

Question Number	Container / Receptacles	Answer Choice	Write your answer here
1	Carton	A	
2	Jug	J	
3	Cask	B	
4	Urn	E	
5	Punnet	D	
6	Wardrobe	G	
7	Flask	C	
8	Wallet	H	
9	Library	I	
10	Sheath	F	

EXERCISE 71: CONTAINERS / RECEPTACLES

Match the each of the following containers with their corresponding items.

A. Wine	B. Fruit	C. Uniform	D. Beer	E. Letter
F. Documents	G. Flowers	H. Keys	I. Sword	J. Jam

Question Number	Container / Receptacles	Answer Choice	Write your answer here
1	Keg	D	
2	Bowl	B	
3	Envelope	E	
4	Carafe	A	
5	Kitbag	C	
6	Jar	J	
7	Briefcase	F	
8	Handbag	H	
9	Scabbard	I	
10	Vase	G	

EXERCISE 72: SOUNDS

Match the each of the sound to the appropriate creature.

| A. Screams | B. Brays | C. Howls | D. Chatters | E. Sings |
| F. Cackles | G. Squeals | H. Quacks | I. Bleats | J. Trumpets |

Question Number	Name of the Creature	Answer Choice	Write your answer here
1	Hyena	A	
2	Duck	H	
3	Lark	E	
4	Elephant	J	
5	Donkey	B	
6	Monkey	D	
7	Hen	F	
8	Rabbit	G	
9	Lamb	I	
10	Wolf	C	

EXERCISE 73: SOUNDS

Match the each of the sound to the appropriate creature.

A. Grunts	B. Hums	C. Squeaks	D. Croaks	E. Neighs
F. Bells	G. Brays	H. Lows	I. Drones	J. Caws

Question Number	Name of the Creature	Answer Choice	Write your answer here
1	Pig	A	
2	Frog	D	
3	Deer	F	
4	Cow	H	
5	Horse	E	
6	Crow	J	
7	Bee	I	
8	Beetle	B	
9	Ass	G	
10	Mouse	C	

Mastering 11+ / VOCABULARY / Practice Book

EXERCISE 74: MOTIONS

Match the each of the motion word to the appropriate creature.

A. Ambles	B. Waddles	C. Lumbers	D. Prowls	E. Lopes
F. Trots	G. Frisks	H. Soars	I. Flits	J. Gallops

Question Number	Name of the Creature	Answer Choice	Write your answer here
1	Lamb	G	
2	Elephant	A	
3	Hyena	D	
4	Wolf	E	
5	Pig	F	
6	Horse	J	
7	Duck	B	
8	Bear	C	
9	Lark	H	
10	Curlew	I	

EXERCISE 75: MOTIONS

Match the each of the motion word to the appropriate creature.

A. Struts	B. Swings	C. Steals	D. Prowls	E. Flutters
F. Swoops	G. Flits	H. Charges	I. Hops	J. Runs

Question Number	Name of the Creature	Answer Choice	Write your answer here
1	Owl	G	
2	Turkey	A	
3	Lion	D	
4	Pigeon	I	
5	Eagle	F	
6	Dog	J	
7	Ape	B	
8	Cat	C	
9	Bull	H	
10	Robin	E	

EXERCISE 76: COUNTRIES and LANGUAGES

Match the country to the main language spoken.

A. Spanish	B. English	C. Hindi	D. Dutch	E. Farsi
F. Arabic	G. French	H. Maori	I. Danish	J. Urdu

Question Number	Name of the Creature	Answer Choice	Write your answer here
1	Mexico	A	Spanish
2	Pakistan	J	
3	India	C	
4	Canada	G	
5	Denmark	I	
6	Netherlands	D	
7	Egypt	F	
8	New Zealand	B	
9	Iran	E	
10	France	G	

EXERCISE 77: COUNTRIES and LANGUAGES

Match the country to the main language spoken.

A. Zulu	B. Yoruba	C. Bengali	D. Gaelic	E. Polish
F. English	G. Russian	H. Finnish	I. Singhalese	J. Cymric

Question Number	Name of the Creature	Answer Choice	Write your answer here
1	Nigeria	B	
2	Poland	E	
3	Russia	G	
4	Finland	H	
5	U.S.A	F	
6	Bangladesh	C	
7	Sri Lanka	I	
8	Wales	J	
9	Scotland	D	
10	South Africa	A	

EXERCISE 78: COUNTRIES and CAPITAL CITIES

Match the country to the appropriate capital city.

A. Edinburgh	B. Rome	C. Beijing	D. Madrid	E. Cardiff
F. Kingston	G. Tokyo	H. New Delhi	I. Warsaw	J. Dublin

Question Number	Name of the Creature	Answer Choice	Write your answer here
1	India	H	
2	Scotland	A	
3	Wales	E	
4	Ireland	J	
5	Italy	B	
6	Jamaica	F	
7	China	C	
8	Spain	D	
9	Poland	I	
10	Japan	G	

EXERCISE 79: COUNTRIES and CAPITAL CITIES

Match the country to the appropriate capital city.

A. Athens	B. Vienna	C. Cairo	D. Copenhagen	E. Amsterdam
F. Berlin	G. Helsinki	H. Harare	I. Canberra	J. Bern

Question Number	Name of the Creature	Answer Choice	Write your answer here
1	Switzerland	J	
2	Egypt	C	
3	Denmark	D	
4	Netherlands	E	
5	Greece	A	
6	Germany	F	
7	Zimbabwe	H	
8	Australia	I	
9	Finland	G	
10	Austria	B	

Mastering 11+ / VOCABULARY / Practice Book

EXERCISE 80: COUNTRIES and CURRENCIES

Match the country to the appropriate currency.

A. Ruble	B. Euro	C. Yen	D. Dinar	E. Krona
F. Rand	G. Pound	H. Krone	I. Yuan	J. Dollar

Question Number	Name of the Creature	Answer Choice	Write your answer here
1	Belgium	B	
2	Iceland	E	
3	South Africa	F	
4	Japan	I	
5	Jersey	G	
6	Australia	J	
7	Norway	H	
8	China	C	
9	Russia	A	
10	Iraq	D	

ANSWERS

Mastering 11+ / KS2 Vocabulary

www.mastering11plus.com/answers
for updates and clarifications on answers

All queries via email to: enquiry@mastering11plus.com

ANSWERS:

EXERCISE 1		EXERCISE 2		EXERCISE 3		EXERCISE 4		EXERCISE 5	
1	G	1	G	1	G	1	H	1	B
2	H	2	B	2	A	2	C	2	C
3	A	3	D	3	C	3	A	3	J
4	F	4	J	4	J	4	F	4	D
5	J	5	H	5	B	5	G	5	E
6	B	6	C	6	I	6	B	6	A
7	E	7	F	7	D	7	J	7	H
8	C	8	I	8	F	8	D	8	I
9	D	9	A	9	E	9	E	9	G
10	I	10	E	10	H	10	I	10	F

EXERCISE 6		EXERCISE 7		EXERCISE 8	
1	Radii	1	Appendices	1	Witnesses
2	Churches	2	Sheep	2	Aircraft
3	Geese	3	Mice	3	Storeys
4	Deer	4	Crises	4	Flies
5	Children	5	Fungi	5	Shelves
6	Fish	6	Criteria	6	Wives
7	Axes	7	Media	7	Tornadoes
8	Oases	8	Oxen	8	Tomatoes
9	Summaries	9	Matrices	9	Zeroes
10	Lives	10	Formulae	10	Calves

EXERCISE 9		EXERCISE 10		EXERCISE 11	
1	Passers-by	1	Bacteria	1	C
2	Cupful(s)	2	Diagnoses	2	J
3	Pence	3	Moose	3	A
4	Reefs	4	People	4	B
5	Pianos	5	Dice	5	D
6	Dwarves / Dwarfs	6	Data	6	H
7	Knives	7	Lassos / Lassoes	7	I
8	Echoes	8	Trout	8	E
9	Charities	9	Geniuses / Genii	9	G
10	Sisters-in-law	10	Phenomena	10	F

EXERCISE 12		EXERCISE 13		EXERCISE 14		EXERCISE 15		EXERCISE 16	
1	J	1	G	1	A	1	C	1	G
2	C	2	B	2	H	2	B	2	B
3	A	3	D	3	B	3	A	3	A
4	D	4	I	4	F	4	I	4	C
5	B	5	A	5	J	5	J	5	E
6	F	6	C	6	I	6	D	6	F
7	E	7	H	7	D	7	F	7	H
8	I	8	E	8	G	8	H	8	D
9	H	9	F	9	C	9	G	9	I
10	G	10	J	10	E	10	E	10	J

ANSWERS:

EXERCISE 17		EXERCISE 18		EXERCISE 19		EXERCISE 20		EXERCISE 21	
1	G	1	I	1	B	1	E	1	J
2	D	2	B	2	H	2	C	2	H
3	J	3	G	3	D	3	J	3	A
4	A	4	A	4	E	4	G	4	F
5	C	5	D	5	A	5	A	5	E
6	I	6	J	6	J	6	H	6	B
7	F	7	C	7	I	7	D	7	G
8	B	8	H	8	F	8	F	8	D
9	E	9	E	9	C	9	I	9	C
10	H	10	F	10	G	10	B	10	I

ANSWERS:

EXERCISE22		EXERCISE 23		EXERCISE 24		EXERCISE 25	
1	D	1	F	1	believe	1	persistent
2	E	2	B	2	tomorrow	2	unfortunately
3	J	3	C	3	aggression	3	supersede
4	G	4	J	4	argument	4	occurring
5	H	5	H	5	accommodate	5	tendency
6	C	6	G	6	chauffer	6	liaise
7	I	7	D	7	embarrass	7	irresistible
8	F	8	E	8	ecstasy	8	humorous
9	A	9	A	9	necessary	9	harassment
10	B	10	I	10	cemetery	10	independent

ANSWERS:

EXERCISE 26		EXERCISE 27		EXERCISE 28		EXERCISE 29		EXERCISE 30	
1	C	1	H	1	A	1	E	1	I
2	H	2	C	2	H	2	A	2	F
3	A	3	A	3	B	3	C	3	D
4	B	4	B	4	F	4	B	4	C
5	F	5	I	5	J	5	F	5	B
6	J	6	D	6	D	6	J	6	H
7	G	7	E	7	C	7	D	7	G
8	D	8	F	8	E	8	G	8	E
9	E	9	G	9	I	9	I	9	J
10	I	10	J	10	G	10	H	10	A

ANSWERS:

EXERCISE 31		EXERCISE 32		EXERCISE 33		EXERCISE 34		EXERCISE 35	
1	H	1	C	1	D	1	F	1	F
2	A	2	A	2	F	2	D	2	A
3	D	3	J	3	C	3	H	3	E
4	C	4	D	4	J	4	I	4	C
5	B	5	I	5	I	5	A	5	I
6	E	6	H	6	H	6	G	6	D
7	F	7	F	7	G	7	J	7	G
8	G	8	E	8	E	8	C	8	H
9	J	9	B	9	B	9	E	9	J
10	I	10	G	10	A	10	B	10	B

ANSWERS:

EXERCISE 36		EXERCISE 37		EXERCISE 38		EXERCISE 39		EXERCISE 40	
1	H	1	B	1	H	1	H	1	H
2	A	2	A	2	A	2	C	2	A
3	C	3	E	3	D	3	I	3	F
4	D	4	H	4	F	4	D	4	B
5	F	5	C	5	C	5	E	5	G
6	I	6	G	6	B	6	A	6	J
7	E	7	D	7	G	7	B	7	C
8	B	8	J	8	I	8	F	8	I
9	G	9	F	9	J	9	G	9	D
10	J	10	I	10	E	10	J	10	E

EXERCISE 41		EXERCISE 42		EXERCISE 43		EXERCISE 44		EXERCISE 45	
1	J	1	E	1	C	1	J	1	A
2	H	2	C	2	F	2	I	2	I
3	G	3	B	3	E	3	H	3	E
4	E	4	D	4	H	4	G	4	D
5	C	5	G	5	B	5	F	5	C
6	D	6	H	6	D	6	E	6	F
7	F	7	J	7	I	7	D	7	B
8	I	8	I	8	J	8	C	8	H
9	B	9	A	9	A	9	B	9	G
10	A	10	F	10	G	10	A	10	J

EXERCISE 46			EXERCISE 47		
Question	Answer Choice	Compound Word	Question	Answer Choice	Compound Word
1	E	**QUADRANT**	1	A	**KNOWLEDGE**
2	A	TRIPLET	2	B	DOWNLOAD
3	H	STIRRED	3	H	UPHELD
4	**B**	RAMPANT	4	**D**	BACKGROUND
5	G	GRIDLOCK	5	J	ANTHEM
6	I	HANDSOME	6	C	POSTAGE
7	F	FORECAST	7	F	INJURY
8	C	JUSTICE	8	G	FOREFRONT
9	D	BUTTERCUP	9	I	OUTLET
10	J	CARTRIDGE	10	E	FORTUNE

EXERCISE 48			EXERCISE 49		
Question	Answer Choice	Compound Word	Question	Answer Choice	Compound Word
1	I	**ATTEMPT**	1	C	**RESTORE**
2	F	FORWARD	2	G	FOREMOST
3	H	TEASING	3	A	INCONSIDERATE
4	**C**	PORTABLE	4	B	THOUGHLESS
5	B	WITHER	5	E	OUTLAW
6	D	INFRINGE	6	J	WILDLIFE
7	E	OUTLYING	7	H	BEHOLD
8	A	MAYHEM	8	D	POPPIES
9	J	GREENHORN	9	F	SUBDIVISION
10	G	BEETROOT	10	I	MISTRUST

ANSWERS:

EXERCISE 50			EXERCISE 51		EXERCISE 52	
Question	Answer Choice	Compound Word	Question	Answer	Question	Answer
1	A	**FORTRESS**	1	**G**	1	**A**
2	C	HALLMARK	2	A	2	G
3	D	STRONGHOLD	3	I	3	E
4	H	BACKFIRE	4	J	4	D
5	F	INADEQUACY	5	H	5	J
6	B	CARPET	6	C	6	H
7	J	CHINWAG	7	E	7	I
8	I	PARDON	8	B	8	B
9	E	CHITCHAT	9	F	9	F
10	G	INKJET	10	D	10	C

EXERCISE 53		EXERCISE 54		EXERCISE 55		EXERCISE 56	
Question	Answer	Question	Answer	Question	Answer	Question	Answer
1	F	1	J	1	G	1	B
2	A	2	G	2	H	2	D
3	D	3	H	3	E	3	D
4	E	4	A	4	A	4	D
5	J	5	I	5	J	5	B
6	G	6	B	6	B	6	D
7	I	7	E	7	C	7	B
8	H	8	C	8	D	8	E
9	B	9	F	9	I	9	E
10	C	10	D	10	F	10	A

EXERCISE 57		EXERCISE 58		EXERCISE 59		EXERCISE 60	
Question	Answer	Question	Answer	Question	Answer	Question	Answer
1	B	1	B	1	E	1	D
2	B	2	D	2	D	2	B
3	D	3	B	3	C	3	B
4	A	4	E	4	E	4	C
5	D	5	B	5	B	5	E
6	C	6	B	6	B	6	C
7	C	7	A	7	C	7	C
8	C	8	D	8	A	8	E
9	E	9	B	9	D	9	E
10	D	10	C	10	A	10	C

ANSWERS:

EXERCISE 61		EXERCISE 62		EXERCISE 63		EXERCISE 64	
Question	Answer	Question	Answer	Question	Answer	Question	Answer
1	H	1	E	1	F	1	A
2	E	2	B	2	E	2	B
3	G	3	F	3	J	3	C
4	A	4	D	4	I	4	D
5	B	5	A	5	B	5	F
6	D	6	J	6	C	6	J
7	J	7	H	7	A	7	E
8	I	8	C	8	G	8	I
9	F	9	I	9	H	9	G
10	C	10	G	10	D	10	H

Mastering 11+ / VOCABULARY / Practice Book

ANSWERS:

EXERCISE 65		EXERCISE 66		EXERCISE 67		EXERCISE 68	
Question	Answer	Question	Answer	Question	Answer	Question	Answer
1	E	1	C	1	D	1	F
2	B	2	A	2	H	2	A
3	J	3	E	3	A	3	B
4	F	4	J	4	E	4	E
5	C	5	B	5	J	5	D
6	H	6	F	6	C	6	C
7	G	7	H	7	F	7	J
8	D	8	G	8	G	8	G
9	I	9	I	9	I	9	H
10	A	10	D	10	B	10	I

ANSWERS:

EXERCISE 69		EXERCISE 70		EXERCISE 71		EXERCISE 72	
Question	Answer	Question	Answer	Question	Answer	Question	Answer
1	E	1	A	1	D	1	A
2	J	2	J	2	B	2	H
3	D	3	B	3	E	3	E
4	I	4	E	4	A	4	J
5	A	5	D	5	C	5	B
6	F	6	G	6	J	6	D
7	G	7	C	7	F	7	F
8	B	8	H	8	H	8	G
9	H	9	I	9	I	9	I
10	C	10	F	10	G	10	C

Mastering 11+ / VOCABULARY / Practice Book

EXERCISE 73		EXERCISE 74		EXERCISE 75		EXERCISE 76	
Question	Answer	Question	Answer	Question	Answer	Question	Answer
1	A	1	G	1	G	1	A
2	D	2	A	2	A	2	J
3	F	3	D	3	D	3	C
4	H	4	E	4	E	4	B
5	E	5	F	5	F	5	I
6	J	6	J	6	J	6	D
7	B	7	B	7	B	7	F
8	I	8	C	8	C	8	H
9	G	9	H	9	H	9	E
10	C	10	I	10	I	10	G

EXERCISE 77		EXERCISE 78		EXERCISE 79		EXERCISE 80	
Question	Answer	Question	Answer	Question	Answer	Question	Answer
1	B	1	H	1	J	1	B
2	E	2	A	2	C	2	E
3	G	3	E	3	D	3	F
4	H	4	J	4	E	4	C
5	F	5	B	5	A	5	G
6	C	6	F	6	F	6	J
7	I	7	C	7	H	7	H
8	J	8	D	8	I	8	I
9	D	9	I	9	G	9	A
10	A	10	G	10	B	10	D

Other books in the Mastering 11+ series:

- ➢ English & Verbal Reasoning – Practice Book 1
- ➢ English & Verbal Reasoning – Practice Book 2
- ➢ English & Verbal Reasoning – Practice Book 3

- ➢ Cloze Tests – Practice Book 1
- ➢ Cloze Tests – Practice Book 2
- ➢ Cloze Tests – Practice Book 3

- ➢ Maths – Practice Book 1
- ➢ Maths – Practice Book 2
- ➢ Maths – Practice Book 3

- ➢ Comprehension – Multiple Choice Exercise Book 1
- ➢ Comprehension – Multiple Choice Exercise Book 2
- ➢ Comprehension – Multiple Choice Exercise Book 3

- ➢ CEM Practice Papers – Pack 1
- ➢ CEM Practice Papers – Pack 2
- ➢ CEM Practice Papers – Pack 3
- ➢ CEM Practice Papers – Pack 4

All queries to **enquiry@mastering11plus.com**

Printed in Great Britain
by Amazon